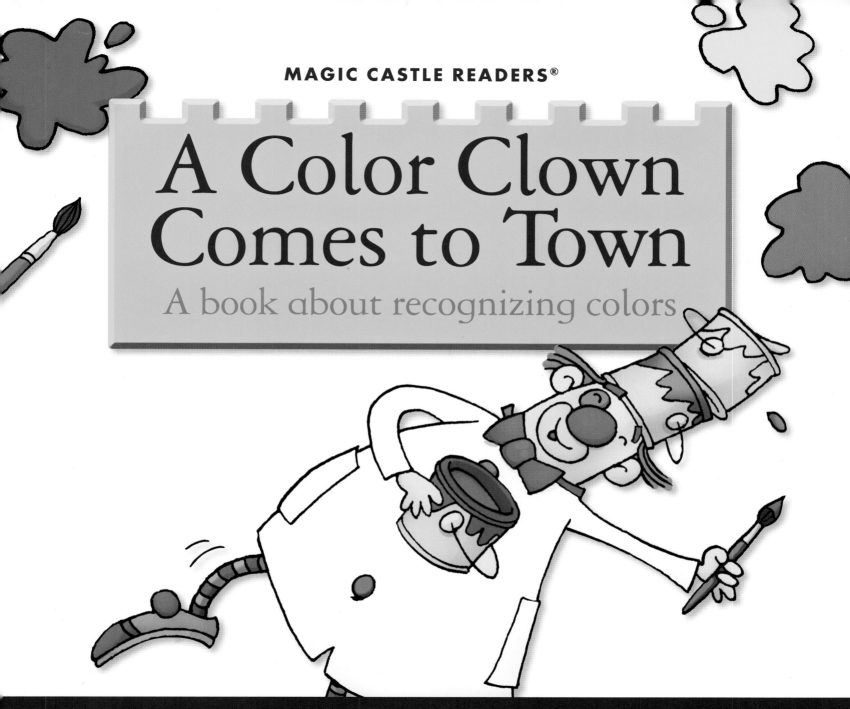

A Color Clown Comes to Town

A book about recognizing colors

BY JANE BELK MONCURE • ILLUSTRATED BY PATRICK GIROUARD

The Child's World®

Published by The Child's World®
1980 Lookout Drive • Mankato, MN 56003-1705
800-599-READ • www.childsworld.com

Acknowledgments
The Child's World®: Mary Berendes, Publishing Director
The Design Lab: Design
Jody Jensen Shaffer: Editing

ISBN 9781623235659
LCCN 2013931407

Printed in the United States of America
Mankato, MN
July 2013
PA02177

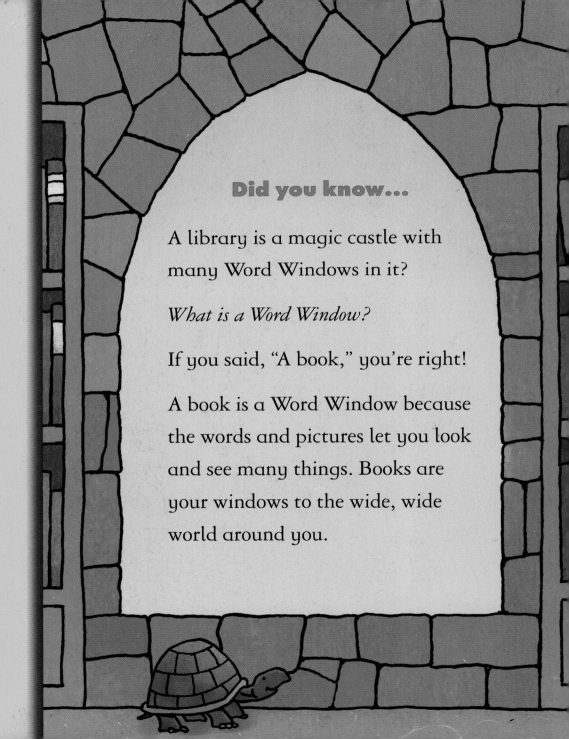

Did you know...

A library is a magic castle with many Word Windows in it?

What is a Word Window?

If you said, "A book," you're right!

A book is a Word Window because the words and pictures let you look and see many things. Books are your windows to the wide, wide world around you.

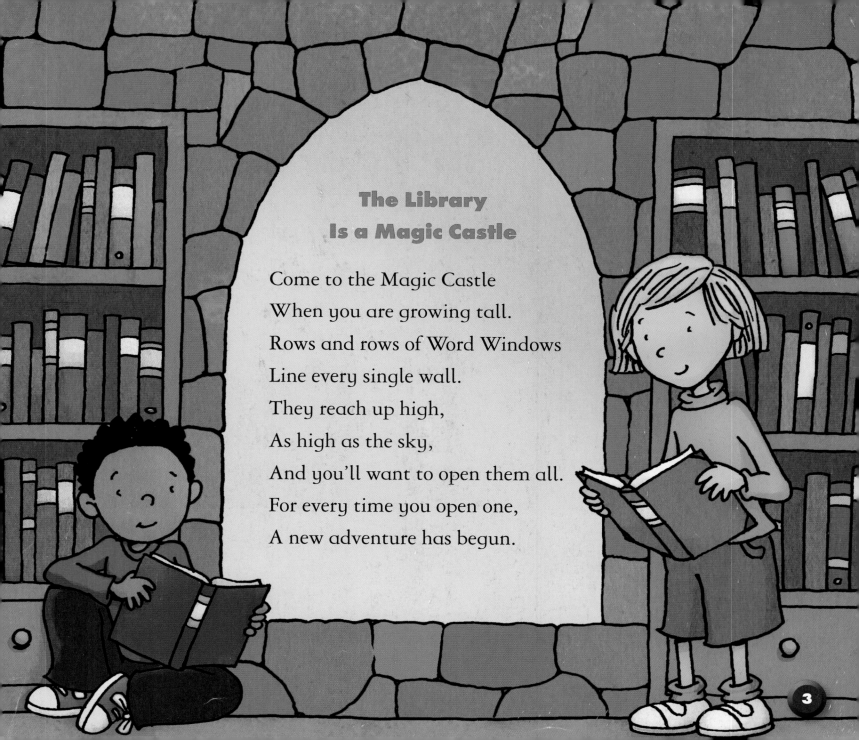

The Library Is a Magic Castle

Come to the Magic Castle
When you are growing tall.
Rows and rows of Word Windows
Line every single wall.
They reach up high,
As high as the sky,
And you'll want to open them all.
For every time you open one,
A new adventure has begun.

Emma opens a Word Window.
Guess what she sees. A funny clown.

"I am the Color Clown," he says.
"I paint things all over town. You can paint, too."

Color Clown takes the red bucket off his head.
"Let's paint something red," he says.

Color Clown finds a polar bear.
"Let's paint the bear."

"No," says Emma.
"I never saw a red polar bear.
We cannot paint the polar bear red."

Emma finds a toy fire truck.
Can you paint a fire truck red?
They do. They paint it. It looks like new.

"Now let's paint something blue,"
says Color Clown.

Color Clown finds an igloo.

"No," says Emma.
"I never saw a blue igloo.
We cannot paint the igloo blue."

Emma finds a toy car. Can you paint a car blue?
They do. They paint the car. It looks like new.

"Now let's paint something yellow,"
says Color Clown.

Color Clown finds a snowman in the snow.

"No, no, silly fellow. A snowman
is never yellow," says Emma.

Emma finds a toy steam shovel.
Can you paint a steam shovel yellow?
They do. They paint it. It looks like new.

"Now what can we do?" asks Emma.
"I will do tricks," says Color Clown.

Color Clown mixes red with yellow.
What new color does he make?

"I can paint something orange," says Emma.
What does she paint?

"Can you do another trick?" asks Emma.

"Yes," says Color Clown.
He does a flip.

Then Color Clown mixes yellow and blue.
What new color does he make?

"I can paint something green for you," says Emma.
What does Emma paint?

"Can you do another trick?" asks Emma.

"Yes," says Color Clown.
He stands on his head.

Then Color Clown mixes blue with red.
What new color does he make?

"Now I can paint something red, yellow, orange, blue, green, and purple for you," says Emma.

Emma paints a rainbow.

"Good-bye, Color Clown," says Emma.
"It is time to go. I must close this Word Window."

Emma paints a rainbow at home. Can you?

Questions and Activities

(Write your answers on a sheet of paper.)

1. Describe the two characters in the story.
   Write two things about each one.

2. Did this story have any words you don't know?
   How can you find out what they mean?

3. What does it mean when Emma says the clown is a silly fellow?
   How do you know it means that?

4. How does the clown make the color orange?
   Why did the clown not mix yellow and blue to make orange?

5. Name two things you learned about mixing colors.
   What else would you like to know?